The Story of Jesus

By Jane Werner Watson

Illustrated by Jerry Smath

Revised Edition

A GOLDEN BOOK · NEW YORK

Copyright © 1977, 2000, 2002 by Penguin Random House LLC.
All rights reserved. Published in the United States by Golden Books, an imprint of
Random House Children's Books, a division of Penguin Random House LLC,
1745 Broadway, New York, NY 10019, and in Canada by Random House of Canada,
a division of Penguin Random House Ltd., Toronto. Originally published in 1977 in
different form by Western Publishing Company, Inc. Golden Books, A Golden Book,
A Little Golden Book, the G colophon, and the distinctive gold spine are registered
trademarks of Penguin Random House LLC.
randomhousekids.com
Educators and librarians, for a variety of teaching tools, visit us at
RHTeachersLibrarians.com
Library of Congress Control Number: 2006923667
ISBN 978-0-375-83941-2
Printed in the United States of America
Revised Edition 2007
36 35 34

Jesus was born in Bethlehem, a town in the rocky hills of Judea. Mary and Joseph were his parents.

Joseph worked as a carpenter. When Jesus
grew old enough, he helped him.

Jesus was twelve years old when he and his parents went to Jerusalem for the feast of Passover. Jesus was thrilled by the sight of Jerusalem towering behind its great stone walls.

Jesus's heart rejoiced when he entered the temple, the house of the Lord God. Jesus knew, even then, that his life's purpose would be to work for his Father in Heaven, telling people about Him.

When Jesus became a young man, he met a prophet called John the Baptist. John asked people to stop doing wrong and to be baptized to show that they were starting a new and better life.

John baptized Jesus in the River Jordan. At that moment, God sent a dove down from Heaven—a sign that He was pleased.

Afterward, Jesus went off by himself, deep into the desert. He stayed for many days, thinking about the good and evil in the world. He prayed for God to show him the way to live his life.

When Jesus returned from the wilderness, he began to teach. He traveled from town to town, preaching the good news of the Kingdom of God and healing those who were sick.

Jesus met with fishermen
tending their nets on the shore . . .

and with shepherds
watching their flocks.

Once, Jesus spoke to a crowd of about five thousand people. It grew late and everyone was hungry. Only one boy had brought food—five loaves of bread and two small fishes.

Jesus took the boy's food and blessed it. Then he broke the food into pieces and gave it to the people. Through Jesus's miracle, everyone had enough to eat.

One night when Jesus and his disciples were
on a boat, a terrible storm blew up. The men were
terrified, but Jesus called out, "Quiet! Be still!"
The storm stopped, and the waves died down. This
was another one of Jesus's miracles.

Jesus often walked through vineyards
and fields, teaching the people by telling
them stories about people like themselves.

He told stories about workers gathering grapes in the vineyards, as Jesus gathered people to God. He told them about shepherds searching for lost sheep, as God searched for sinful people, hoping to change their ways. . . .

Jesus told people to follow the wishes of God rather than worry about becoming wealthy. He pointed to the flowers of the field, which do not worry about wealth or work for it. Yet God clothed them in greater beauty than wealth could ever buy.

But not everyone liked Jesus. The leaders of the temple were afraid that Jesus would turn the people against them. They were glad when a man named Judas offered to lead them to Jesus. The temple leaders paid Judas thirty pieces of silver.

Soon Jesus was captured by a group of soldiers. They brought him before the governor, a man named Pontius Pilate. When Judas saw this, he was sorry for what he had done to Jesus. He tried to return the money to the leaders of the temple, but it was too late.

Pontius Pilate let the soldiers take Jesus away to a place called Golgotha. There he was crucified with two other men. Before he died, Jesus prayed to God. "Forgive them," he said. It was a sad day for all the people who loved Jesus.

Three days later, some women visited
Jesus's tomb. They were surprised to find an
angel waiting for them. "Don't be afraid," the
angel said. "Jesus has risen! He is not here."
And soon Jesus appeared to the women
himself, on the road.

Just before Jesus went up to Heaven, he appeared to his disciples and told them to travel to faraway places and teach people to obey his words.

"And I will be with you always," promised Jesus, "until the end of the world."